new decor design

daab

New Decor Design explora las propuestas más contemporáneas del diseño y la arquitectura residencial. Con el objetivo de proporcionar una perspectiva amplia del interior de cada vivienda, el libro muestra diferentes ejemplos de lofts, apartamentos, casas unifamiliares y espacios rehabilitados que aseguran una percepción global de cada estancia. En el interior los juegos de luz y color se convierten en los protagonistas del espacio y los muebles crean zonas de circulación que enfatizan la distribución del espacio. Ya no es necesario seguir una determinada tendencia; la vivienda actual es versátil, singular y experimenta con las formas y los materiales para crear un espacio cómodo y bien resuelto. Los proyectos presentados a continuación, obra de arquitectos de renombre internacional, son una prueba de la habilidad para generar una nueva arquitectura interior en esta última mitad de siglo.

New Decor Design explore les propositions les plus contemporaines du design et de l'architecture résidentielle. Dans le but de fournir une ample perspective des intérieurs de chaque demeure, l'ouvrage expose différents exemples de lofts, appartements, maisons individuelles et espaces rénovés qui assurent une perception globale de chaque pièce. Dans les intérieurs, les expériences de lumières et de couleurs deviennent les acteurs principaux de l'espace et les meubles créent un cheminement mettant en valeur leur distribution. Il n'est plus nécessaire de se soumettre aux modes; la demeure actuelle est multifonctionnelle, singulière et novatrice tant avec les formes qu'avec les matériaux, afin de créer un espace confortable et bien conçu. Les projets présentés ici, œuvres d'architectes de renommée internationale, démontrent les capacités à générer une nouvelle architecture d'intérieur au cours du demi siècle passé.

New Decor Design esplora le proposte più contemporanee del design e dell'architettura residenziali. Al fine di fornire un'ampia prospettiva dell'interno di ogni abitazione, il libro mostra diversi esempi di loft, appartamenti, case unifamiliari e spazi ristrutturati che assicurano una percezione globale di ogni stanza. All'interno gli esperimenti di luce e colore diventano i protagonisti dello spazio, e gli arredi creano un dinamismo che accentua l'effetto della distribuzione. La casa attuale è versatile, singolare e sperimenta con forme e materiali. Non è necessario fare riferimento a tendenze determinate ma si cerca semplicemente una buona soluzione spaziale per vivere con comodità. I progetti presentati di seguito, opera di architetti di fama internazionale, sono una prova dell'abilità di generare una nuova architettura degli interni in questa ultima metà del secolo.

New Decor Design erkundet die modernsten Vorschläge im Bereich der Innenarchitektur und Wohnhausarchitektur. Um dem Leser einen möglichst umfassenden Überblick über Einrichtungsmöglichkeiten für Wohnhäuser zu bieten, werden in diesem Band verschiedene Beispiele von Lofts, Wohnungen, Einfamilienhäusern und anderen Arten von Umbauten gezeigt, die einen globalen Eindruck jeder dieser Wohnungen vermitteln. Das Spiel mit Licht und Farbe verwandelt sich in den Protagonisten des Raumes und die Möbel schaffen eine Dynamik, die die Raumaufteilung betont. Es ist nicht mehr notwendig, sich auf Trends zu berufen: der heutige Wohnraum – vielseitig und einzigartig – experimentiert mit den Formen und Materialien um einen angenehmen und gut gestalteten Raum zu schaffen. Die gezeigten Umbauten und Einrichtungen sind Werke international anerkannter Architekten und beweisen ein großes Talent und die Fähigkeit, eine neue Architektur zu schaffen.

New Decor Design explores the most contemporary proposals in residential design and architecture. With the aim of providing a wide perspective of each home's interior, the book shows different examples of lofts, apartments, houses and renovated spaces, which guarantee a global perception of each place. Lighting and color selections are the main determinants of the overall feel of an interior space, while furnishings reinforce the layout and even create secondary circulation paths. The design of the modern home is distinguished by its flexibility and individuality, but not that it necessarily follows any stylistic trends. Experimenting with form and material, contemporary design is concerned with creating well thought-through, commodious living spaces. The projects presented, works from internationally renowned architects, are testimony to the ability, over the last half-century, to generate a new interior architecture.

Agustí Costa | Barcelona, Spain
Duplex in Berga
Berga, Barcelona, Spain | 2005

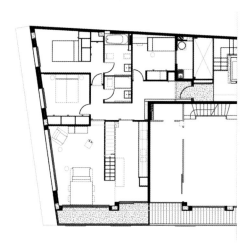

Air Projects | Barcelona, Spain
Loft Vapor Llull
Barcelona, Spain | 2005

Air Projects | Barcelona, Spain
Reina Victòria Apartment
Barcelona, Spain | 2003

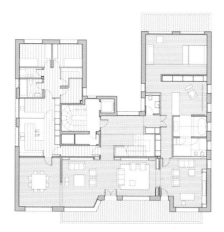

Arantxa Garmendia, David Maturen | Zaragoza, Spain
Penthouse in Barcelona
Barcelona, Spain | 2001

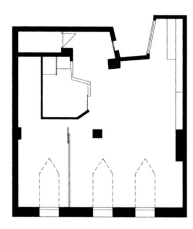

Avi Laiser & Amir Shwarz | Tel Aviv, Israel

Loft Ben Avigdor
Tel Aviv, Israel | 2005

B5 Architecten/Dieter van Everbroek | Gent, Belgium
Architecture of Removal
Gent, Belgium | 2005

BANG — Bureau d'Architectes Nicolas Gouygou | Brussels, Belgium
Loft Berthelot
Forest, Belgium | 2005

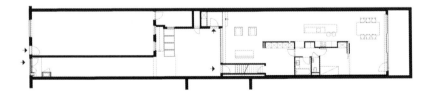

Bea Mombaers | Knokke, Belgium
Chez Nous
Knokke, Belgium | 2005

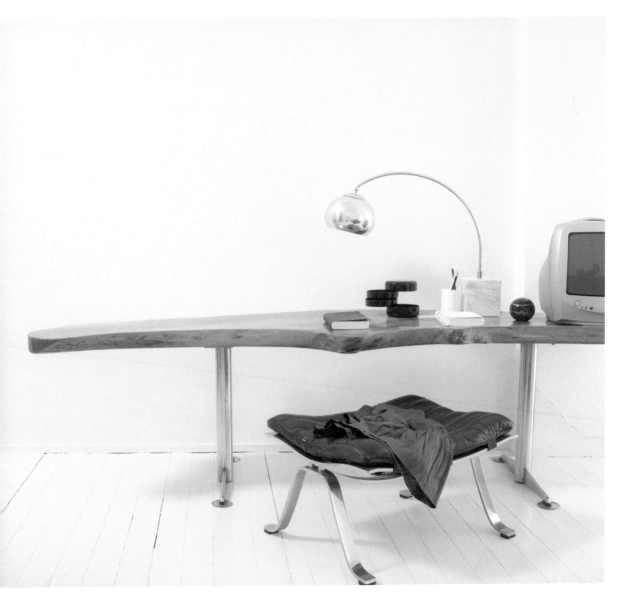

Cloud 9 | Barcelona, Spain
Villa Bio
Llers, Girona, Spain | 2004

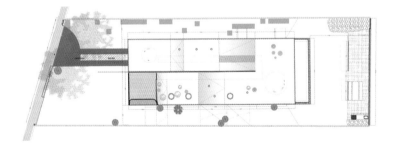

Eduard Samsó | Barcelona, Spain
Duplex in Sarrià
Barcelona, Spain | 2005

Esther Gutmer (Decoration), Olivier Dwek | Brussels, Belgium
Loft Bodson
Brussels, Belgium | 2005

Filippo Bombace | Rome, Italy
House in Colosseo
Rome, Italy | 2006

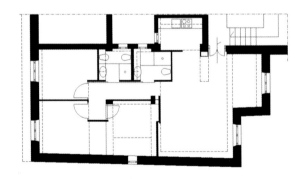

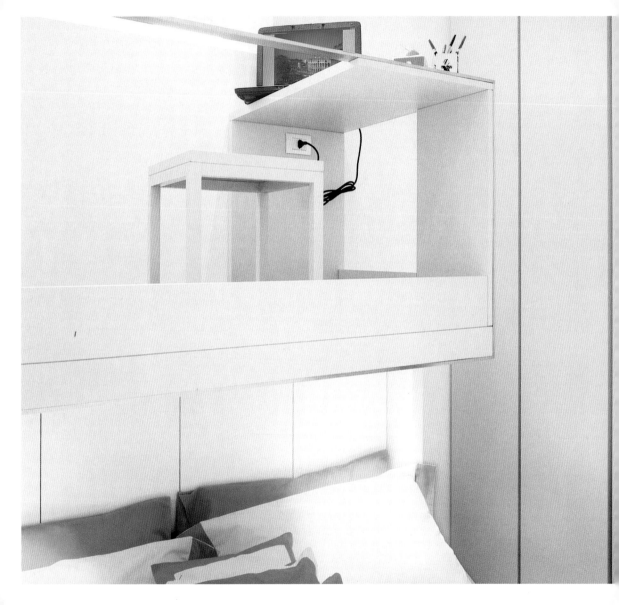

Filippo Bombace | Rome, Italy
Laura House
Rome, Italy | 2006

Gus Wüstemann | Zürich, Switzerland
Glacier Loft
Lucerne, Switzerland | 2005

Johannes Will | Vienna, Austria
Fassangasse Apartment
Vienna, Austria | 2004

La Granja Design | Barcelona, Spain
Hevia House
Sant Cugat del Vallès, Spain | 2005

Martínez Lapeña-Torres Arquitectes | Barcelona, Spain
Ibiza House
Ibiza, Spain | 2005

Resolution: 4 Architecture | New York, USA
The Loft of Frank & Amy
New York, USA | 2004

Saadvanced/P. Mora, M. Sánchez-Bedoya, L. Martín y Aznar | Guadalajara, Spain
Studio-House in Guadalajara
Guadalajara, Spain | 2004

-CASA.

erti en hombre. Primero tuve que convertirme en mujer.
o había sido neutra, no era en absoluto una mujer.
rque si entras en una reunión de hombres, profesional o no,
etrero diciendo: ¡MIRA! ¡TENGO TETAS!; siempre se
s murmullos y esos rubores y ese retorcerse en el asiento
y ese abrocharse los botones y las alusiones y cortesías
oinada con las insinuantes insistencias respecto a mi físico:
dez para agradarme. Si logras ser Uno de Los Chicos
te, implica cierta despersonalización, pero el letrero desaparece:
ida y me reía de los chistes verdes, sobre todo de los hostiles.
iciendo cortés pero firmemente no, no, no, no, no,
trabajo y me gusta mi trabajo. Supongo que decidieron
a mejor calidad; o que no eran reales, o que pertenecían
a), así que contaron conmigo sólo del cuello para arriba;
spersonalización (...) No soy una mujer; soy un hombre.
a de mujer. Soy una mujer con mente de hombre.

Russ.

DE LA RUINA AL POLVO

PARK
LABEL

you can find
inspiration
in everything

Inspiration can be found in everything...

DE LA RUINA AL

las

lo discontinuo

Cristales votos brillan en la Carretera

Cada persona se inventa una manera propia de atravesar el bosque

HE intentado llegar de un punto a otro, sin poner los pies en el suelo.

Instrucciones para doblar una puerta, una ventana o cualquier otro objeto doméstico.

Objetos doblados con hidráulicos

Maquetas en *madera* astillada

Studio Marginet | Gent, Belgium
James Bond on 38 m^2
Gent, Belgium | 2001

Agustí Costa
Plaza de la Creu, 3, 2.ª 2.ª
08600 Berga (Barcelona), Spain
P +34 938 211 063
F +34 938 221 105
estudi@agusticosta.com
Duplex in Berga
Photos: © David Cardelús

Air Projects
Pau Claris, 179, 3.º 1.ª
08037 Barcelona, Spain
P +34 932 722 427
F +34 932 722 428
www.air-projects.com
Loft Vapor Llull
Reina Victòria Apartment
Photos: © Jordi Miralles

Arantxa Garmendia, David Maturen
Santa Isabel, 3, ático
5003 Zaragoza, Spain
P +34 976 392 407
F +34 976 399 895
arantxigarmendiao@hotmail.com
davidmaturen@hotmail.com
Penthouse in Barcelona
Photos: © Jordi Miralles

Avi Laiser & Amir Shwarz
6 Meytav Street
67898 Tel Aviv, Israel
P +972 3 562 5440
F +972 3 562 1639
avilaiser@hotmail.com
Loft Ben Avigdor
Photos: © Miri Davidovitch

B5 Architecten/Dieter van Everbroeck
Beukenlaan 22
9051 SDW, Gent, Belgium
P +32 9 385 53 59
F +32 9 321 07 59
www.B5architecten.be
Architecture of Removal
Photos: © Vercruysse & Owi/Dujardin

BANG — Bureau d'Architectes Nicolas Gouygou
Rue Egide van Ophem 108
1180 Brussels, Belgium
P +32 2 370 46 50
F +32 2 370 46 92
www.archi-bang.org
Loft Berthelot
Photos: © Laurent Brandajs

Bea Mombaers
Kustlaan 289
8300 Knokke, Belgium
P +32 50 603 606
F +32 50 603 611
items@skynet.be
Chez Nous
Photos: © Owi/Verne

Cloud 9
Pasaje Mercader, 10, bajos 3.ª
08008 Barcelona, Spain
P +34 932 150 553
F +34 932 157 874
www.e-cloud9.com
Villa Bio
Photos: © Luis Ros

Eduard Samsó
Tallers, 77, ático
08001 Barcelona, Spain
P +34 933 425 900
samso@coac.net
Duplex in Sarrià
Photos: © Jordi Miralles

Esther Gutmer (Decoration)
Avenue des Klauwaerts-laan 27
1050 Brussels, Belgium
P +32 2 648 25 00
F +32 2 648 18 06
Loft Bodson
Photos: © Laurent Brandajs

Filippo Bombace
Via Isola del Giglio 3
00141 Rome, Italy
P +39 068 689 8266
www.filippobombace.com
House in Colosseo
Laura House
Photos: © Luigi Filetici

Gus Wüstemann
Köchlistrasse 15
8004 Zürich, Switzerland
P +41 1 295 60 10
F +41 1 295 60 19
architects@guswustemann.com
Glacier Loft
Photos: © Zapaimages.com/Bruno Helbling

Johannes Will
Seidlgasse 41/5
A-1030 Vienna, Austria
P +43 1 718 03 78 11
F +43 1 718 03 78 19
www.willl.at
Fassangasse Apartment
Photos: © Paul Ott, Graz

La Granja Design
Ciutat de Granada, 28 bis, 3.º
08005 Barcelona, Spain
P +34 933 568 405
F +34 933 568 406
www.lagranja.it
Hevia House
Photos: © Luis Hevia

Martínez Lapeña-Torres Arquitectes
Roca i Batlle, 14, 1.º
08023 Barcelona, Spain
jamlet@arquired.es
Ibiza House
Photos: © Jordi Miralles

Olivier Dwek
34 Avenue Brugmann
1060, Brussels, Belgium
P +32 2 344 28 04
F +32 2 344 28 00
dwek.architectes@gmail.com
Loft Bodson
Photos: © Laurent Brandajs

Resolution: 4 Architecture
150 West 28th Street Suite 1902
New York, NY 10001, USA
P +1 212 675 9266
www.re4a.com
The Loft of Frank & Amy
Photos: © Reto Guntli/Zapaimages.com

**Saadvanced/Pedro Mora, Marta Sánchez-Bedoya,
Luis Martín y Aznar**
Crta. GU-254, km 3,5
19114 Moratilla de los Meleros (Guadalajara), Spain
P +34 949 38 87 17
F +34 949 38 87 73
www.saadvanced.com
Studio-House in Guadalajara
Photos: © Luis Hevia

Studio Marginet
Geneviève, Ronny (Jerom) & Léon Duquenne
Baudelostraat 31
9000 Gent, Belgium
P +32 9 324 91 90
James Bond on 38 m^2
Photos: © Owi/Vercruysse & Dujardin

© 2007 daab
cologne london new york

published and distributed worldwide by
daab gmbh
friesenstr. 50
d - 50670 köln

p + 49 - 221 - 913 927 0
f + 49 - 221 - 913 927 20

mail@daab-online.com
www.daab-online.com

publisher ralf daab
rdaab@daab-online.com

creative director feyyaz
mail@feyyaz.com

editorial project by loft publications
© 2007 loft publications

editor marta serrats
layout ignasi gracia blanco
english translation jay noden
french translation michel ficerai / lingo sense
italian translation maurizio siliato
german translation susanne engler
copy editing cristina doncel pablo

printed in china

isbn 978-3-937718-73-6